GRIEF MATTERS:
Authentic Perspectives of Life and Loss

Anthology created by:

Dr. Shanelle Fields, LPC

Vera Brown, LPC, CGC

Dr. Laganna Lawrence

Esaunta Buncomb

Deidra Addison

Acknowledgements

We would like to thank our families, friends and loved ones for allowing us the opportunity to speak the truth about grief. It is one of the most difficult and strenuous parts of life; however, it is a path we must all walk and experience. Through it all, we have been able to turn our pain into a greater purpose by comforting, educating, and supporting others in their time of need.

Table of Contents

Permission to Grieve

Our world has experienced a great deal of loss in the past few years. There have been numerous deaths due to the Covid-19 virus. Some of these we had to time to prepare for. Others were gone in what seemed like a split second. And to some, we never got to say goodbye.

We lost family and friends in Brooklyn, NY, and Uvalde, Texas, due to hurt and pain that was never comforted or healed. Parents will never take that child to school again and grandchildren will never be able to celebrate another birthday with their grandparent ever again.

Senseless gun violence takes lives every single day. Ages young and old, are losing loved ones at alarming rates. It is unbearable to think about.

To this end, we are giving you the Permission to Grieve! This anthology seeks to let you know you don't have to be strong. You can cry! You can yell! You can scream! Grief is a process. Let's walk this journey together.

Stages of Grief

Denial: *Not believing or acknowledging the loss of a loved one (ex.- Did this really happen?)*

Anger: *Negative feelings about losing a loved one (ex.- Being mad at the world or others due to the loss)*

Bargaining: *Using an exchange of something in life to bring back the deceased loved one (ex. I will stop partying if (deceased loved one) comes back)*

Depression: *Feelings of extreme sadness, isolation, doubt, worry (ex.- Not sleeping or eating; stopping normal activities)*

Acceptance: *Acknowledgment of death (ex. It hurts so badly, but I know he/she isn't here anymore.)*

(Kubler Ross, 1969)

Stages of Grief Symptoms

(WHAT AM I FEELING?)

Denial: In this first stage, there is disbelief and the opposite of acceptance. Symptoms include frustration, worry, doubt, fear, and apprehension.

Anger: This is the stage where negative emotion surfaces. It is characterized by outbursts, short temper, mistrust of the world and the search for someone or something to be mad at.

Bargaining: At this moment, there is a feeling of offering or doing whatever is necessary to bring the loved one back. These may include extreme measures.

Depression: This stage affects every part of daily life. There may be changes in eating habits of having no appetite to overeating. Interest in doing fun things or hanging out with friends may be a lost cause.

Acceptance: *The last stage essentially means acknowledging, coming to terms with, creating a new normal, and learning to live without the deceased loved one.*

**It takes many people a great deal of time to get to this place. **

(Kubler-Ross, 1969)

Life After Death

Ok Ok...before I get started, let me put this disclaimer out... "this will NOT be your ordinary chapter dealing with grief!" You might laugh and cry and that is okay! We ALL need to acknowledge the hurt we are going through; whether the loss was recent or 20 years ago...it still has changed who we used to be. So, with that being said...

1. This is a safe place!
2. Allow yourself to be in the moment and know that you are NOT alone! Now that we have that out the way...

WELCOME! Come on in...take a load off! You're probably thinking what in the world is she talking about? I'm reading a book. I know that! In this chapter, we're going to talk about what most people don't talk about...but everybody is thinking...LIFE AFTER DEATH! I don't mean the Notorious B.I.G. album for my music lovers, and I also don't mean what the ones we have lost experience either. I AM TALKING ABOUT THE GOOD OL' FASHION, picking up the pieces of your life after you have experienced a loss. Whether expected or not...you still may be trying to figure out what's next. Did you know how your life was going to change after that loved one passed away? Did anybody tell you what to expect for the days/months/years ahead? Still have no clue? Let me help you. I'm talking about after the last guest leaves, after you have read the last sympathy card, smelled the last condolences flower, ate the last piece of food that has been brought in, and the last family member that was in town for the funeral has decided to leave. You know that feeling that comes and makes you realize that this feeling is for real? That's what we are going to talk about.

For me, it's the "New Beginning" and every time you lose a loved one, something changes. Some people expect you to just pick up the pieces and carry on and it's never that easy! Death already doesn't come with a manual, no chapters to read to handle grieving. Now here we are, trying to process a situation where we have no choice but to start over. Losing someone you love and care about never gets easier and some losses are harder to handle than others, but one thing for sure is that it's not impossible. You must allow yourself to go through the motions. Allow yourself to grieve over the loss. Too many times we just try to shake grief off. We try to go back to our regularly scheduled programs, not realizing that in due time, our body is like "hold up...wait a minute...so are we just going to act like we didn't lose somebody we cared about?! We are hurting and we are tired carrying on like it never happened, therefore we are shutting down." If you never heard your body say that to you but you are someone who tries to pick up the pieces...then bless your heart...it is coming! Ever had a moment where it's the middle of the day and tears begin to fall when you hear a song? How about smelling a scent that automatically triggers a memory of that person? Oh, let's not go to cars! When my brother passed away, I started to notice more

Chevy Silverado's in my area! And you know what, EVERYTIME I saw a black one...my mind ran immediately on him. I plan to get one to honor him...sounds crazy? (Aht aht...this is a judgment free zone).

Ever hear a phrase that reminds you of that person? I know most of you are like...YESSS; I've been there! It doesn't matter when the loss was either. Every time I go in the grocery store and see chicken feet (yes...I'm from the south), I remember my grandmother and a story she told me one day while I was helping her shop (aht aht...don't you talk about my sweet ol' granny either)! She's been dead for 24 years! It's those cries and/or screams in the shower or tub when you are trying to deescalate from the day or trying to rejuvenate for the morning. It's those rides in the car when you are supposed to be going to a destination, but your mind wanders off and begins to reminisce about the times you have spent with the person. HELLO SOMEBODY! I know! Sometimes we try to be so strong for EVERYBODY else; we neglect ourselves! We try to mask what has happened and what is happening. Are you wondering how so? You don't even know me to tell me what I'm doing! I know grief! I have experienced losses! I have learned that life after death was something real even as a child! I remember I lost my grandmothers...in less than a year of each other...that was hard! They were such a part of my life and my routine on a weekly basis; on top of other expectations that life was sending my way. I had to say...wait I need to talk to somebody who knows what I'm going through. Knowing what I know now, I see that as a child I was more open to receiving help while I was experiencing grief. As an adult, I feel as though people may not KNOW what to say when you are grieving and therefore the average person grieves in silence and that bothers me. We can sit here and discuss all day about what people should or should not say to someone who is grieving but that needs to be a book by itself! We can also discuss the time that people gather to the house to offer their condolences, but they stay all day. Thank you, Sister Mae, for staying with us all day but we promise you...AT NIGHT...is when our grief really sets in! We do not know whether we are COMING or GOING! To me, the easy part is up to the funeral and even all of that can be hard. Once that loved one is in the ground, reality sets in but you still don't acknowledge it because maybe you have guests around, maybe people are even staying at your house to honor that lost loved one, maybe your job only gave you 3 bereavement days...nonetheless LIFE AFTER DEATH has started and we are NEVER prepared. Some of you are probably yelling at me right now how you have your wills and life insurance policies located in the China closet with the list of all your valuable documents... yea not talking about that. We're talking about being mentally, physically, emotionally ready to grieve. You are like how am I supposed to do that? You don't! Tell me, did you find it easier to grieve knowing that loved one was going to pass away or losing them suddenly? Probably neither. If grief hits everybody different each time, how can we be prepared? I remember watching both my parents lose their mothers, siblings, other relatives, friends, some were unexpected while other deaths they knew were coming; but what shook them the most...was the loss of their son. Nobody could have prepared them for that! Death still hurts!

So, knowing that the loss of a loved one and the grief that comes along with it is inevitable and will look different each time...how can we help each other with life after death? By telling you...it is okay to not know what your new life will look like. It is okay to even tell people who truly genuinely love you (not the nosey ones that are secretly glad it's you and not them) that you are NOT OKAY! Seeking help...we must get out of the mindset of talking to a counselor/therapist is taboo and you will go to hell for talking.

If we only surround ourselves with people who are experiencing the same loss and all we're doing is discussing the loss without any actions...guess where we'll always be? Stuck at part 1 of grieving. Do not isolate yourself completely but do NOT feel that you ALWAYS have to be out in the crowds...monitor and adjust. Grief is like a rollercoaster, allow yourself to experience the highs and the lows; however, make sure to get a support system to help you as you adjust. Don't be stubborn and stuck in your ways, if we don't do better with how we handle grief we will be a sealed box full of emotions bursting at the seams until we explode.

If you are reading this book, you are off to a great start! Here's some encouraging words to wrap up our session...Keep going! Never give up! Remember the good times! Know that love never dies and, in those moments, where you feel like the grief is too much to bare, think about something that you enjoy doing that will be a release for you...a way to lift your spirits, call a friend/family member who will just sit on the phone and listen to you scream out loud, or come sit with you in the silence. And finally, we all need someone as we grieve...you don't have to be alone!

Am I Dreaming?

Grief is random and unexpected. Nothing can prepare you for it. It can tear your world apart.

My first encounter with death had to be my great grandfather. I can say that I grieved because I didn't understand death at that point. All I know is that I was sad mainly because everyone around me was. I wouldn't count that as a grudge point, but it was the beginning. My grandmother (his daughter) never spoke as to why we needed to head down the dirt road. We used to walk barefoot to and kick sand just because we liked the way it felt between our toes. This day we would be greeted with the smell of a wooden tobacco pipe that laid between my grandfather's lips. Instead, we were met by an ambience of ambulances and a burn smell that left nothing good to the nostril. My grandfather had fallen to a horrible death by fire. He was burned alive trying to burn the shrubs from the debris in his yard. What's vivid to me is nothing more than sitting in the dark green Chevrolet waiting for my grandmother to come back to the car. I didn't understand, not even the day of the funeral. The remains of him were so grim that it was a closed casket and a picture of remembrance laid on the top.

When I was only twelve years old, I hadn't experienced any more pain than a fall from my bike, mosquito bites or the rips on my backside when I misbehaved as a child. Even though I was exposed to other things, my mother was very particular on what she allowed. On weekdays, I would be home with her and on weekends I would more than likely be in the country with my grandparents. This was so they could keep a watchful eye, while she continued to work a part time job. Summer was well spent in the presence of my grandparents, who were the epitome of my family. I was more than happy to see the smiles on their faces when I arrived. I can only imagine they also felt the same; the company would be great for the empty nesters to have us come to help around the house. Most mornings, I would wake up to the humming of gospel while my grandmother rummaged through and aligned the chores for the day. I was held accountable to a very strict routine of cleaning house and yard work. It began to bother me less, knowing at the end of the day, I would be rewarded with a nice dinner, hot bath, and a few hours of the wheel of fortune. I didn't take any day for granted when I spent time with my grandparents, of course I knew, one day I wouldn't have the opportunity to be with them. This summer seemed to be the best. My family and I went on our normal family trip. We spent more time at the country house than normal. When summer finally was over, we went back to our normal routine during the week school and work. At the end of every school day, I would rush off the bus to call my grandmother to give the highlights of the day or to fill her in on how much I missed her and was ready for the weekend. As usual, as the week ended, we prepared for church every Sunday. My family would meet after church for dinner. My grandmother would always have a feast for the family. I can't remember the entire meal, but I do remember that peach cobbler; it was all I could do that day to finish my dinner to dive into it. We ended that night with our goodbyes; my grandmother walked us to the gate waving as if she was saying her last goodbye. We all replied with our simple, "See you later we love you."

I was awakened the next morning by the sound of the rain beating on the raggedy window of our apartment. It had been raining that night on and off into the morning. My mom came to me as if she had just lost her best friend. She said, "Come on we have to go see grandma; your grandad just called to say she wasn't feeling well, and we should go now." I'm always excited to go see grandma, but I had no idea what this time would be like. My legs were stiff, and I couldn't move. My mom got the car ready for us to leave. It was about a 30 min drive, but it took us about 20 minutes, no less. My grandparents lived in a wooded area and my mother was driving so swiftly, the trees looked as if they were losing their leaves. I often wonder if that was my grandmother waving goodbye as the wind was bringing them along with the car. My mother was silent all the way there. I dared to say a word because if I had known her, I knew she could also tell this call was different. At the beginning of the road to my grandparent's house, there was a ray of sunlight so bright it washed the rain away for just a quick second. There was a down pour as we got closer to the driveway. I could see the cars on the side of the road as we vastly approached. Once I saw the ambulance and a white van, I knew something was terribly wrong. My mother rushed in the yard, barely putting the car in park. She left me in the back seat as I had been slowly getting out of the seat belt, not understanding the urgency. I saw the sadness in my family as I approached the house door. Then, I glanced at my younger cousin who lived in the house with my grandparents. She was on the couch crying but was quickly startled at the running and screaming of my mother, "NOOOOOOOO Momma why you left me?""

I can't say this has been a long-term belief, but I can say that I do believe in "The Broken Heart Syndrome." I would consider this to be the time when the loved one is grieving and appears to have moved on in life. I believe people who have been together for a long period of time have the same effect on each other in life and death. I do feel that it's possible for people to have loved so deeply that they don't want to leave the other behind, so even in death there is an emotional attachment. At some point, the loved one feels they may not want to live without the other; therefore, the person who is left gives up on the human form of life. My maternal grandfather was this way, and we all knew how he felt about my grandmother. She was a queen in his eyes, and he did everything he could to care for and protect her. I honestly don't think my grandmother really knew what the inside of a grocery store looked like because my grandfather did all the shopping. He was a strong man, but she was his weakness. My grandparents had been married over twenty years, had five children, and had not spent any nights without each other unless my grandfather worked the graveyard shift at the cement plant. Other than being at the house or masonic hall, that's where he faithfully dedicated his time. So, if he was ever absent then there had to be a valid reason and so this day there was. If I could think correctly, my grandfather was scheduled to be to work for the graveyard shift the night before. It could've been his alternate week to do mornings; however, my uncle who has been working alongside him since getting out of high school, got the message that my grandfather was a no show. This raised concerns since my grandfather was a precise man and his time was very important to him. My uncle tried to contact him several times before going to the house to check on him, but there was no answer. I am not sure where I was exactly when I got the news, but what I do know is my uncle found my grandfather in his favorite recliner with a bowl of butter pecan ice cream and grapes. His death caught all of us by surprise because, yet again, my grandfather was active and we knew he missed my grandmother, who was his first love. We just didn't know how much. When my family went in to clean his room, they were all taken back from what they saw. For all these years, my grandfather was sleeping in the bed with my grandmother's obituary. He wasn't as good as we thought he was, but he was good at hiding the pain. The day of her funeral, my grandfather was sitting in the front row. When we walked to the casket, he never moved. I happened to take a glance at him, and to this day I still can see that he had no expression; he was in shock. At first, I didn't know what to think because everyone was so heartbroken, but now I see his heart was broken as well. He didn't act this way at his mother's funeral as he got up to speak over her and rejoiced. For his wife, there was a different type of love, and he had his own way of grieving. This was by placing the obituary near him every night. That also makes me wonder if he was just waiting to go be with her again. Did he grieve so much about losing her that he just gave up and prayed for GOD to take him too? I guess we will never know.

My next loss was different; this was someone that I had a relationship with for a few years. He wasn't living the best life, but I loved him and respected his choice for how he chose to live his life. I just couldn't understand a man with his ability and experience making the decisions that he made. It could have been that he was grieving himself but used it as a cover up to get past his own pain. He watched his father make the same mistakes but instead of learning from them, he used it to heal. This is only my perception of it because I wouldn't want to put myself in a situation knowing the consequence would only lead to death. I thought all those things as I walked to his casket straddling my one-year-old son on my right hip. It felt like I was walking miles to get there, and my feet were getting heavier and heavier the closer I got. The floors seemed to be caving under my feet as if I was about to sink in. There he laid as beautiful as the day we met, life foolishly taken from a senseless act or possibly jealousy. I ask myself was it worth that or was it the pain that he was feeling that caused him to ignore all the signs. Not even two months prior, he was robbed and still refused to take the proper precaution. To this day, I still don't, and I doubt I will ever understand. I concluded that he came into my life for a reason, and it was that same reason that he was now gone. I too could have been laying in a casket for my family to view, but I chose to love him from afar. The pain I had endured from this same person is also the person who taught me the same hustle tactic I use today. (If it is beneficial to you, get what you need from it and move on and don't stay too long). When he comes to me in a dream the next day, I try to figure out what message he was trying to send me. Has he forgiven me for leaving and making my life better without him or is that a sign of peace? I used to cry after moments like this, but I don't anymore. I felt that I grieved him when he was alive.

My paternal grandfather stood about 6 feet or more ever since I can remember. When I think back, there was no wonder I was the only one in my class at the age of 8 who was pushed to the back of the line, and always asked to reach the top of the cubby holes due to my height. Every time I would see him pull up in his white work truck, I couldn't wait for him to stop. He would pick me up to kiss me and tickle me with his beard that smelled of Irish Spring soap. He was a very successful man and very devoted to the local schools and community. No wonder I was so caught off guard when my auntie had to come to South Carolina to move him to Kentucky when his health started to decline. Diabetes and hypertension had run its course over the years for the once lover of animals and farm life. It took some adjusting to see my grandfather with his limbs amputated because of the diabetes. I could tell that he wasn't comfortable with the chances of becoming disabled. His living arrangements were soon limited from being independent to depending on others to make decisions on how he would be cared for. If I had the chance to sit with my grandfather, I am almost certain that he would tell me that he didn't want to live his life that way and he would also tell me how hard of an adjustment it was to him.

I can remember driving to my mother's house, my phone rings, my father is on the other end. I can tell something isn't right by the silence; then he speaks calmly and softly just enough to push the information over the phone waves. He says, "Your grandfather just passed." I immediately felt numb. I felt a warm tear drop slide down my cheek as I forced my car to stay in the right lane. I couldn't speak for what felt like two whole minutes. I just remember asking him if he was okay, and he said I will be fine. I just wished I had been there five minutes sooner to say my goodbyes. I don't know if it was because my grandfather had two funerals, where he once lived and the other where he was born, but the day of the funeral I wasn't emotional. I had been dealing with my mother's illness for the last few years and I was exhausted. I had taken too many losses and the effects that they had on me were indescribable to what I was feeling that day. I do think of my grandfather often, especially when I have accomplished certain things in my life, but I smile instead of crying.

The death of my mother is still unparalleled; nothing can compare to the loss of the only person who has ever known me. I don't know if I have or if I will ever accept her death. I have blamed myself so much for not being able to spend as much time as I wanted to with her during her sickness. But what could I have done when I was the primary caregiver to her and my children? Who do I turn to when she is depending on me to keep it all together for us? I don't give myself time to think about it much, but I do believe I was going through a process of grieving when she was sick. I think this is why I am responding to it differently or why I feel numb to some degree. I was able to see the physical change in my mother. Since she always felt sorry for herself, I think there is a piece of me that is at peace due to the fact that she is no longer suffering, and I took care of her the best I could. I also know that her mental status would not have been good going through Covid. I often think that if she had lived until this time, she would have mentally exhausted herself, and given up on trying to get better, although she would have been home, where she was loved and supported. We all tried our best to give my mother a normal life. Day by day, she became more depressed with her situation. She felt that she was a burden, when in fact, I'm glad I had the opportunity to care for her. She had been there for me all my life and if it wasn't for her, I would've had to put my career on hold.

The day my mother passed, I only cried once when the doctors came in to tell me there was nothing else they could do. I was in denial; I don't know if it was because I felt we had been there before, and she had recovered, or if I was just trying to convince myself that this was just a dream, and at any moment, I would wake up. In hindsight, I believe my mother was gone the day she went to the doctor and never returned and not the day I was asked to take her off life support. Clearly, it was those two weeks that I was given to come to terms with what was going to happen. My grieving was every single day. I sat in the waiting room with the smell of anesthesia waiting to hear my mother speak to me again. It wasn't until the day that I walked behind my mother's casket that I realized that there is no dream to wake up from, just the reality of what is yet to come. My mother, my best friend, will no longer physically be here.

Will I ever really understand what it is to grieve? Even when I thought I was coping, I felt like I was being judged. So, I only allowed myself time to be in that space when there was nothing else going on around me, or I would talk to others that were going through the same things I had experienced. Some of those people ended up hurting more than helping. Some just felt like grieving was no good and we should move past the pain and move forward in life. In those conversations, I realized I was conflicted. My grief brought both pleasure and pain. I had to be the one who determined what it meant to me and how I was going to overcome or fix it.

Even when I do get love and support, I still feel dismissed especially with family, which is why I stopped talking to them about it. My pain has been reduced to yearly death anniversary calls and short I love your texts. I was confused and lonely; at some point, I just decided that so much was happening that I didn't have time to grieve. I started to pretend that everything was fine instead of having to explain my grief to others that didn't understand. I knew I needed help, but I didn't know what kind of help to ask for. I still have a void in my life for where I am now and where I want to be. I have a normal pain inside of me that can't be explained through any life experience. All I can do is respond with skill and grace to try and clean it up and put it behind me. What is grief when most of it is carried inside of us? I was once chewed out for feeling that another person would be unhappy at their loss. To my concern, it had no effect on her at all, which also changed my outlook on what grieving can really mean because some people resent death and are held captive to their own beliefs. All of these events affected me in one way or another, but I can't say for sure when I allowed myself to grieve during the process.

I have a tendency of becoming numb to situations, especially those I have no control over. As a person who has grieved and studied people who have grieved, I have found that none of us have ever come up with one single way on how to truly handle grief. As a result, we don't know how to be helpful. It's my observation that grief should be seen and treated as a realistic thing. Our lives have been changed by loss, and we must find a new way to move on without our loved one. I have been on both sides of grief. I know what it feels like to want to lay in bed for days, not eat and not talk to anyone. I've also listened to the different aspects of grief in my client's lives. I have learned to never talk anyone out of their pain, but to be attentive instead. *With all this experience and recent studies, the question still remains......... Did I ever give myself permission to grieve?*

Anticipatory Grief is a Real Thing

As a youngster, I may have first heard the word *grief* in the phrase "good grief Charlie Brown." However, as I began to grow older, my next encounter with grief was probably after the loss of a loved one. What is grief? I am so glad you asked. Grief my friend is something no one is envious of; it often takes a seat front and center of individual lives. Grief shows up in its own time and space and stays around for varying lengths of time. Grief can be viewed as the reaction exemplified when there is any kind of loss. Typically, when individuals speak of grief, it is in reference to a loss by death. Grief is the loss of someone or something that is important to you.

Do you recall your first encounter with grief? My first encounter with grief, bereaved or bereavement was around the age of 12. It was the year that I attended the funerals of my maternal great grandfather, paternal great grandmother, maternal grandfather, and maternal step- grandfather, all in one year. It was also the year Dr. Martin Luther King, Jr., whose picture was on our dining room wall, was assassinated. It was the year I heard the song "When I've Gone the Last Mile of The Way" for the very first time, a song that serves as a grief trigger to this day (Last Mile, 2016). It seemed like the world had stopped for each of the adults around me. Unaware of what I felt at the time; I also had an early encounter with grief when my Auntie and Uncle (Mom's sister who was married to Dad's brother), as a military family, moved across country from South Carolina to Sacramento, California taking my double cousins! Oh, how I cried that day as the Rambler pulled out of Big Mama's yard with some of my favorite people in that car! Big Momma's words to me were, "stop crying before you cry them away," meaning they could be gone forever if I continued to cry. As cliché as that may have sounded even then, I believed it as if it were the gospel and I subdued those tears, just as we instruct grieving individuals to subdue their emotions today. We often tell grieving individuals to 'stay strong, your loved one would not want you to cry, you have to be strong for the children, the spouse, or whomever is the next of kin.' I clearly remember my moments of anger, inappropriately expressing that anger and moments of trying to comfort others, with no knowledge of what was taking place emotionally in my world or theirs. Yet, I wanted to comfort the adults whose pain I witnessed. I realize now that I displayed the traits of being a helper even back then.

Being the only child in the home, is probably when the fear of death, the fear of losing a loved one became instinctively inherent. Losing a loved one due to military travels, losing a loved one through a temporary hospital stay or vacation or through death, became a deeply dreaded emotion. Most detrimental and frightening was the fear of losing my parents. With there being only three people in the house, how could we afford to lose one or God forbid, lose two. That horrendous fear manifested itself increasingly as the years went by and as I experienced the loss of every female (maternal great grandmother, two grandmothers and many aunts who had been instrumental spiritually, emotionally, and physically in my growth and development into the woman I had become. Thankfully along the way I had been introduced to Jesus and found comfort in the knowledge of HIS redeeming grace, the knowledge that my loved ones who had preceded me, all had a personal relationship with the Father who had promised eternal life. I found comfort in the words of **Romans 10:9 ...** that if you confess with your mouth the Lord Jesus and believe in your heart that God has raised Him from the dead, you will be saved as well as in **Romans 10:13** For "whoever calls on the name of the Lord shall be saved (NKJV Romans 10:9 and 13, 1982)."

The grief that I encountered at an early age was primarily due to the death of a loved one. However, life's lessons have taught us that there are so many diverse types of losses that allow grief to show up. The loss of a job, home, pet, relationship, or even transitioning from home to college or college life back home are scenarios that may bring about feelings of grief. Life's lessons and academic lessons have also taught that there are distinct types of grief. Diverse types of grief include, abbreviated grief, absent grief, anticipatory grief, chronic grief, collective grief, complicated grief, delayed grief, disenfranchised grief, distorted grief, exaggerated grief, inhibited grief, masked grief and lastly, normal grief (Types of Grief). I strongly recommend that you research the meaning of each type of grief mentioned. At any given time, it may prove to be helpful in recognizing the distinct types of grief you or someone you know may be dealing with.

The type of grief I intend to address specifically in this section of my journey is anticipatory grief. Sometimes described as stress or anxiety, it in fact may be actual symptoms of anticipatory grief. It is the expectation or anticipation of a loss, due to illness which may or may not qualify as terminal illness. Chronic illnesses that are debilitating may also lend to anticipatory grief due to the loss of independence and quality of life. Anticipatory grief could also refer to the expected loss of a relationship. I am here to confirm that anticipatory grief is a real thing. Fear and apprehension surrounding anticipatory grief can be crippling. Sometimes it would immobilize me so badly, I felt like I did not want to go to sleep at night or did not want to get up in the morning for fear of what I would find. I did not want to go on weekend trips or even go home to my house from my duties as a caregiver for the weekend for fear of getting a dreaded phone call to come back due to an emergency. Although I knew without a doubt my loved one was left well cared for by our loving CNA, my brother, my son or my grandsons, upon leaving, I would have to work through these feelings of guilt on a regular basis. The fear would often consume me until I would utilize self-talk to get myself in gear to push forward and be productive doing the one thing that would give me life, give me purpose, and that was counseling others. And let me interject here that truly the Lord must have a sense of humor, because I ended up counseling multiple clients with concerns remarkably like mine. You see I had lost myself, lost "my me" at the beginning of the anticipatory grieving process until I listened to that still small voice. I recognized the fact that we all should continue living life to the fullest and enjoy life abundantly. I recognized the adverse effect that fear was having on me physically, mentally, and emotionally. I acknowledged that God was still in control and there was absolutely nothing I could do to delay or prevent HIS coming for my loved one. I recognized that I needed to find comfort in the word of God through text or through music and that I needed to practice what I preach to my clients as a therapist and especially as a Grief Counselor. None of this eliminated my fears and apprehension, but rather served as coping mechanisms.

Upon hearing the news of a terminal illness, many times we may initially feel the need to have a "death watch"- you know, sit around the bedside, and wait for the inevitable. Well, I am here to tell you DO NOT do it. Go on living, especially when that is exactly what your loved one is doing despite what the doctors may have said. Go on living, especially when your loved one is at peace with the diagnosis, at peace with people and at peace with life itself. The strength, contentment, and peace that a loved one facing death exhibits, is enough to bring a smile to the face of anyone on the sidelines. I find comfort in the morning response of "I feel good! Thank the Lord I have no pain." I find peace in the other caregiver's responses of "he had a good night" neighbors' wave as they pass by and my loved one is sitting in the sun, and he waves back or yells "hey bubba" or "hey baby." I know that the neighbors he acknowledges find comfort in the greeting as well for they certainly question his whereabouts when he is not in view.

Here it is another day at 3:30 am and my dad's cough over the baby monitor wakes me up repeatedly. Vertigo has the room spinning, or so I think. I get up slowly to keep my balance and go to his room to administer cough medicine. He is half asleep and sips as though he is sipping a cocktail while in my mind I am saying 'like really dude,' but instead I say repeatedly "come on drink it all down." I am reminding myself to not get upset because, well you know, he may not be here next year this time, next month this time or next whatever. This is the conflicting thought process day in and day out - wondering what lies ahead.

Thirty minutes later when Dad summons me because he needs to go to the restroom, I remind myself once again of unknowns as vertigo and I agree to get up slowly, get balanced and get the task done. Yesterday's excitement of Dad walking with his walker with standby assistance for the first time in three months, does not resolve me of the what ifs and the thoughts of this time next year or next week or next whatever. Anticipatory grief is a real thing.

Despite the voice in my head telling me to not let the enemy steal my joy, or the voice telling me how amazing God has been to this old man of 89 years and ten months of age with no pain and all the other positive and small victories each day, that other voice slips in that continues to remind me of the next time and the what if's. Although each morning begins with the "thank you Lord" from both of us (after I peep in the room to make sure his chest is going up and down, to make sure he's breathing, and there are more chants of "Lord, I thank you" throughout the day, there are still those other conflicting moments. I often think of what Martha said to Jesus, John 11:17 So when Jesus came, He found that he had already been in the tomb four days. 18 Now Bethany was near Jerusalem, about [a]two miles away. 19 And many of the Jews had joined the women around Martha and Mary, 'to comfort them' concerning their brother. Sounds like the "sitting up" was at their house, which is very familiar to us even today. 20 Then Martha, as soon as she heard that Jesus was coming, went and met Him, but Mary was sitting in the house. 21 Now Martha said to Jesus, "Lord, if You had been here, my brother would not have died; that sounds like faith very well spoken to me even though she was obviously grieved. 22 But even now I know that whatever You ask of God, God will give You" (NJKV John 11:17-22, 1982) So, excuse me well-meaning Saints and Aints, who may ask 'where is your faith?' This is where I put one Baptist finger up and tip toe out of that conversation. For what it is worth, I feel no need, nor am I in a place emotionally to justify my professional or spiritual stance as I anticipate the loss of one very constant person in my entire life. That energy can be used much more efficiently in quality care-emotionally and physically for my loved one and in my own selfcare. Although ones' spiritual faith may be alive and well, anticipatory grief is a real thing, especially when one has seen this movie before. The last time(s) I watched this movie in real-time it did NOT end well. Except for the fact that as believers we know our loved ones will live again. In John 11:25, Jesus said to her, "I am the resurrection and the life. He who believes in Me, though he may die, he shall live. 26 And whoever lives and believes in Me shall never die. Do you believe this?" Martha, the sister of him who was dead, said to Him, "Lord, by this time there is a stench, for he has been *dead* four days." John 11:40 Jesus said to her, "Did I not say to you that if you would believe you would see the glory of God (NKJV John 11:25-25, 40, 1982)?"

At 5:20 am, we are both back to bed, for however long. When morning dawns for us around 8:00 a.m. or 10:00 a.m. thankfully the cycle starts again; a cycle that would be impossible for me without the help of a dedicated CNA, loving family members, caring neighbors, an amazing spiritual support system and lastly, the Hospice Staff of Roper Hospital. Oh dear, let us talk about that word "hospice"! Typically, the word hospice is introduced under very trying circumstances. A time when an unfavorable diagnosis is delivered, a time when negative connotations outweigh the positivity of its available services. Culturally we may have been taught that hospice is a death sentence, a short-lived death sentence that is handed out around the time of a diagnosis. I am sure hospice personnel will confirm that hospice care and hospice timelines are as unique as each patient is. Many have been discharged from hospice care to return home to their families. Some are only admitted to hospice for respite care and return home after caregivers have had a few days for much needed rest or travel. Some may be at home under hospice care for days, weeks, months, or years. Here again however, anticipatory grief becomes a real thing. Many families refuse hospice care simply because of the negative connotation mistakenly attached to the word. Many families suffer through caregiver burnout because of a lack of knowledge, lack of information but primarily because of that stigma - that elephant in the room. Hospice care opens the door of professional care for a loved one as well as emotional and spiritual support for the family & caregivers as well as for the patient.

As the roller coaster ride and the emotional upheaval continues, there are always unexpected triggers that find its way into the psyche. At 8 am when a text message reads that two members of the community have passed away on the same day, a trigger sets anticipatory grief in motion. On the one hand there is sadness, but also a thankful heart the death angel did not knock at the door that is most familiar. As selfish as that may seem, we sigh with relief that we are not the ones actively preparing to sit on that front row of seats that no one envies. As the day wears on after receiving that call, I then want to share the tea with someone near and dear to my heart. I do not want to share with my loved one under the care of Hospice, that another one of his peers have passed on. Why should I ruin his day by being the bearer of bad news? The diagnosis and even today's rain has probably done a good job of that already. He's particularly quiet as he is most days, so it is quite difficult to decipher his feelings and his thoughts; after all he is a man's man who does not complain or murmur, but he simply takes one day at a time.

Despite the grueling side effects of anticipatory grief, peace and comfort can be found when we look for the good in a dire situation, when we are thankful for the small victories and when we are simply grateful. Recognizing that the glass is not half empty, but life is still in the glass whether it is half full or a quarter full. Sip on the joys of what remains in the glass, enjoying every bit of it to the last drop. Continue to build memories with your loved one making opportunities for the things he or she enjoyed in better times. My loved one enjoyed family, he enjoyed being in the presence of family, friends, and his church family. We provided every opportunity for him to experience that joy. He always enjoyed being in fellowship with others and appreciated every encounter, always asking "when is the next cookout?" It has been said, that at the end of life, no one ever said they wished they had spent more time at work, but always wished they had spent more time with family. Although my father worked hard from the age of 12 as a farm hand, and later as a self-employed carpenter, self-employed contractor, and a Charleston County building inspector, he was always a people person. He loves people and people love him. I have vivid memories of him saying these words or singing the song 'The Lord will make a way somehow (Lord Will, 2022)" written by Thomas A Dorsey. My mother, a prayer warrior, taught me how to pray. My dad showed me examples of walking in faith, a blessing even years later when anticipatory grief challenged me time after time. And even though this very real thing called anticipatory grief would often prove to be quite expensive emotionally, I would often receive a phone call, a text, or a sermon that would bring me back to the fact that God is in control and that HE really is "a very present help in the time of trouble." I am eternally grateful for every call, text, visit, meals delivered, prayer, and every act of encouragement during the season of being a caregiver. I am most grateful for my brother who has kept me grounded with his quiet, calm mannerism every time I freaked out about the smallest thing. This journey with anticipatory grief began in 2016 with the first stroke and minimal loss of independence, heightened in 2018 with the second stroke and major loss of independence and hit the ceiling in 2021 with a terminal diagnosis.

Anticipatory grief and STUGS or Sudden Temporary Urges of Grief intensified recently because of losses in the community; the death of cousins, neighbors, friends, children of friends and the list goes on (Bursack, 2022). The deaths seem to come so frequently, the words immortality and mortality comes to my mind often. It comes to mind not as fear but as a reminder of life's reality. A reminder to find peace, enjoy all of God's goodness in the land of the living, to soak up all that life has to offer, enjoy family and friends and most of all maintain a personal relationship with the Father. After all, this life is not a rehearsal and none of us will get out of here alive.

Living Through the Inevitable

PONDERING LIFE AND LOSS

Coming to terms with feelings of loss and making sense of it can be a painful process. When I think about grief, only feelings of sadness and loneliness come to mind. Growing up in Anderson, South Carolina, it was routine for my mother to stop by Johnson Funeral Home on South Fant Street. It was the place that all our family members had their funeral services conducted. I would fearfully follow my mother in to "view the body" of those who she desired to pay her respects to. She would look the person up and down after viewing the flowers all around to see who sent them. She would then sign her name on the book for the family to see that she had come. Prior to departure, she would chat with the owner and workers on her way out. During these times, it was the norm for older relatives to pass away mostly from illnesses that were known and then the occasional unknown heart attacks. It was very rare to hear of a newborn or younger person transitioning during these times. From my point of view, there was a specified age range designated to those who passed away. During the funeral services, I can vividly recall the sadness and outcries from relatives which saddened my heart. It was so customary to support families in their sadness and take food, cards and monetary donations to their homes as a measure of love. Shortly thereafter, everyone would continue to move on with their lives.

Losing a loved one is a highly individual experience; there's no right or wrong way to grieve. Even subtle losses in life can trigger a sense of grief. It wasn't until my adulthood that I realized that grieving could occur in other facets of life. For example, you might grieve after moving away from home, graduating from college, or changing jobs. I learned that whatever the loss, it's personal. How you grieve depends on many factors, including your personality and coping style, your life experience, your faith, and how significant the loss was to you. As a result, I was not ashamed about how I felt or believed that it was only appropriate to grieve for certain things.

DIRECT EXPERIENCES

Nothing prepares a person for being present at the death of a loved one, other than experience and many of us do not have that history. Even if one did have a particular experience, it still wasn't with this person. Even a "planned death" will stir emotions that we may not have anticipated. After all, the disease that leads up to this moment was not planned. My first direct encounter with the inevitable was when I was 15 years old, and we received the call that my father had passed away. It was surreal, he lived in California. I only saw him during the summer months when school was out. Although we were distant in travel, I was still a Daddy's girl. The worst part of it all was not being able to attend his funeral due to financial restraints. Once again, time moved on as if nothing had happened. I felt a void but only temporarily.

As much as I had experienced many physical losses, I had NEVER imagined losing my mother. To my demise, I would endure this unimaginable pain at the young age of 22. Shortly after being the first to graduate from college in my family, my mom was diagnosed with terminal Stage 4 lung cancer. Before, I could blink, there was Hospice and then she was gone.

There are no words to describe the emptiness that I felt. I did not know how I could continue to live. I felt that it was so unfair....my father, now my mother and I was just beginning to live my adult life. Who would walk me down the aisle or help me with my children? I felt disconnected from people, places or things. It felt as if I was walking in a fog, without my bearings in the "real world." I had the added stressor of having Power of Attorney and was thrown into the intensity of making funeral/memorial arrangements. We were told that my mother had 3 months to live. She survived an additional 10 days. No matter how the Hospice team attempted to prepare us, I was never prepared for the reality of what was to come. How could I be grateful that my mother was no longer in pain but selfish enough to still want her back?

HOW DO I MOVE FORWARD?

Everyone grieves in their own way and time frame depending on the personal attachment to what was lost. My supervisor at the time of my loss recommended that I join a grief group. Initially, I was not receptive because I felt that I didn't need it and I was learning to cope on my own in my very busy life. However, I eventually gave in. I would attend the group once weekly. It was comprised of others who had experienced the loss of those close to them from Cancer. We would go around a circle and share our feelings and experiences. During this time, I didn't have much to share as I was so focused on getting to whatever was next on my schedule. As a result, I didn't feel as if I gained anything from attending. I began to wonder if I was weird or was my behavior strange because I didn't appear to grieve like the others. As a Rehabilitation Counselor at that time, I knew that group work can be very difficult at times, especially when discussing something so personal. However, it can also be very empowering and healing. Being around others who share this journey can really help normalize the experience. It's importan t to not allow others **tell you how to feel, and don't tell yourself how to feel either.** Your grief is your own, and no one else can tell you when it's time to "move on" or "get over it." Let yourself feel whatever you feel without embarrassment or judgment. It's okay to be angry, to yell at the heavens, to cry or not to cry. It's also okay to laugh, to find moments of joy, and to let go when you're ready.

People will sit back and watch in judgement of how they think you should be grieving or dealing with the loss. Coming to terms with feelings of loss and making sense of it can be a painful process. Bereavement is a type of grief you experience when you lose a loved one. Everyone grieves in their own way and time frame depending on the personal attachment to what was lost. Grief does not have a deadline. After a tragedy or loss, grief can take time. For some, they seem to get over it quickly, but for others the grief stays around. If one person is still grieving while the other seems to not be, try not to be angry or resentful. Just because someone took less time or more time does not mean they are stronger or weaker. Grief has no deadline. It can go on for years and years, and it can be triggered by obvious and not so obvious things. A relationship can be affected negatively if one partner tries to hurry the other's grieving process. Do not do it. Do not give grief a deadline. Grief is not a single emotion. It is an experience that you feel physically, emotionally, mentally, and/or spiritually when you go through something painful. Each person is affected by grief differently. Even two people who go through the same loss may grieve in different ways. For example, one person might go through grief for longer or be less able to function on a day-to-day basis.

Knowledge Gained

There is no "natural" or "good" way to grieve after a loss. Even if the death was anticipated in some ways, the immediate aftermath may be filled with the impression that it was a total surprise. A person's emotional state does not necessarily become apparent until much later in life. I am now in this stage. The stage of delayed grief. **Delayed grief** is when a person's normal grief response is put off until a later time. A person might be doing this intentionally or without even realizing it.

When a loved one dies, you might be faced with grief over your loss again and again — sometimes even years later. Feelings of grief might return on the anniversary of your loved one's death or other special days throughout the year. These feelings, sometimes called an anniversary reaction, are not necessarily a setback in the grieving process. They are a reflection that your loved one's life was important to you. It is important to understand and expect that we all grieve differently. Even in entire families or cultures, a full outpouring of emotions is normal and expected. For example, in some cultures it is traditional for families to cry openly and spend as much time possible at a funeral (including services, burial and viewing) mourning the loved one who has died. Certain reminders of your loved one might be inevitable, such as a visit to the loved one's grave, the anniversary of the person's death, holidays, birthdays or new events you know he or she would have enjoyed. Even memorial celebrations for others can trigger the pain of your own loss. Reminders can also be tied to sights, sounds and smells — and they can be unexpected.

HELPING OTHERS COPE

If someone you care about has lost a loved one, you can help them through the grieving process. Being genuine in our interactions is reassuring since it is the element of ourselves with which we are most accustomed. Even if it does not seem to help or if the mourning person does not express thanks, taking the effort to be attentive and show real care would be much appreciated. It is common to find oneself at a loss for words or acts to comfort a loved one who is going through a difficult period. It is also critical that you only commit to things that you are positive you can follow through on. You should never back out of a promise to help someone else, even if it's as basic as "let me know if there's anything I can do." It is fairly unusual for individuals to say things like this when their emotions and agendas are at an all-time high, such as during funerals (Walter & McCoyd, 2015). This is often intended to be comforting to the grieving person, even though it may aggravate their grief. However, it is quite unusual for people to get genuine assistance or support when they need it. Also, rather than asking if there is anything you want, you may volunteer to assist with a particular task rather than just asking if there is anything you require. As a result, the individual is more likely to consent to receive assistance. Giving assistance in the kitchen, around the home, or with the children is an excellent example of how you might provide a helpful hand.

Another strategy that you could help them is sharing the sorrows with them. Allow them — even encourage them — to talk about their feelings of loss and share memories of the deceased. Also, do not offer false comfort. It does not help the grieving person when you say, "it was for the best" or "you'll get over it in time." Instead, offer a simple expression of sorrow and take time to listen. Finally, remember to keep in contact. In the months after the death of a loved one, the person who has lost that loved one may feel the most alone. Maintaining contact with them may make them feel safer in the knowing that they are not alone. Furthermore, you may want to consider sending a card or note around the holidays, especially if you find it difficult to enjoy after a loss. It's a wonderful feeling to know that someone is thinking about you and has kept you in mind. Also, continue to offer invites to the bereaved to go out and about. They are not compelled to participate right away, which is completely fine; but they may be thankful for your efforts in the long run.

My experiences have allowed me to accept grief as a mystery to be honored instead of a problem to solve. Grief is a complicated beast. But grief is also fundamental. It's the recovery process of how we mentally and physically deal with the loss of a loved one. **Keep in mind** that we are not alone in this difficult time. Grief is a very strange and complex journey. Healing is very possible, and it will happen. All forms of grief and loss are legitimate and real. Never let anyone say that your grief is "less than" because your grief is different from theirs. Allow yourself to heal in your own way and in your own time. My experiences increased my empathy and understanding of grief and loss. I feel that we still live in a society where not only death, but "loss" is not often discussed, and therefore should not be discussed . My hope is that by sharing my experiences, I can help start a new conversation about the grieving process and normalize all the thoughts, feelings and experiences that one goes through when facing grief and loss no matter how "big", "small" or "intense" they are. "Contrary to what we may have been taught to think, unnecessary and unchosen suffering wounds us but need not scar us for life. It does mark us. "You are allowed to be both a masterpiece and a work in progress simultaneously." -Sophia Bush.

It Still Hurts....

Grief is one of those things that lingers. It is dominant and has control over emotions and feelings. After losing a loved one, time seems to stand still, and the pain grows in intensity. Your heart hurts. It is a feeling like no other. Grief and loss bring big strong men to their knees and reduces the toughest woman to a puddle of tears. It can be equated to having open heart surgery with no anesthesia. Literally, a piece of your heart has been removed from your chest. Pain, sadness, hurt, and emotions are the things that accompany this difficult part of life.

I have chosen to focus on the idea that grief is a process that does not JUST GO AWAY. It is not some fleeting moment in time that vanishes. Grief is long-lasting, intermittent, sporadic, spontaneous, and downright overwhelming. You may ask how it can be all those things. Grief moves how it wants to, when it wants to, and happens to everyone. It makes you second guess your progress. Even when you feel some peace about losing your loved one, a song on the radio, seeing that person's favorite color, a television commercial, hearing simple phrases, or passing by someone who still has the very thing you lost, can trigger an overflow of emotions so strong, you may think you are relieving the moment you lost them all over again. The process of grieving has no set time or moment to appear. The "Waves," as I like to call them, just come.

Sometimes, it's a small wave where only a single teardrop may fall. Maybe a medium sized wave hits you at your knees and you find yourself reliving moments of the past. A big wave will come and bowl you over and leave you crying incessantly and the wound you thought was closed has now been re-opened. And to be quite honest, days, months, and years later, it still hurts.

Grief is feeling like Charlie Brown on a very bad day where the rain cloud follows him wherever he goes. The difference is your rain cloud doesn't seem to go away.

Grief is being angry because you have lost a piece of your heart and not understanding why it had to happen.

Grief is wondering how you will move forward.

Grief is feeling isolated, separated, and left out in a room full of people.

Grief is seeing a hearse drive by knowing what is like to have ridden or driven behind it knowing your loved one was once carried to their final resting place.

Grief is knowing that you are prone to shed tears at the drop of dime for any reason.

Grief is having strong faith but having it shaken because you lost your mother, father, child, grandparent, aunt, uncle, cousin, sibling, best friend or loved one and don't know how to cope with the absence.

Grief is feeling overwhelmed with emotion and not knowing how to control it.

Grief is driving a different way because going your normal route means going by the place that brings back memories or thoughts of the countless times your loved one was there.

Grief is living in the unknown because there are no answers to your questions. Grief is.........living with loss.

One of the myths that has been communicated and past down for years is the notion that you just get over the loss or telling people it is time to move on. This is a farce and not a true statement. Your coping skills get better, and you develop ways of dealing with the pain, but you never get over it. Generationally and societally, we have been taught to be strong. As a therapist, I see clients for grief counseling after they are debilitated. When I see them, extremes have set in. They are not eating or sleeping. Their pain is consuming them. Work is difficult. The people around them are not cognizant or understanding about their feelings. In session, I give clients the permission to grieve. I give them the space to cry, to scream, to curse, to question a higher power, and to release some of their pain. Learning the ins and outs of grief was something I had to experience for myself. I thought I had an idea of what grief was, but it wasn't until I lost my best friend, my mother, that I began to truly understand the immense toll her absence had on my life, but there was purpose in my pain. People think they understand grief until it happens to them.

One of the first things that had to change was my thought process, and I had to develop a new routine. I talked with my mother every day for 45 minutes on my drive to work for almost 3 years. It was our ritual. We talked about all the things going on in our lives. She was my secret keeper, my prayer warrior, my safe place and my gentle encourager. How could I begin to start my life over without her? How could I raise my son without her soft instruction and innovative ways to deal with "Little People," as she called them? She was my first call. I can remember going to dial her number only to be reminded that she wouldn't be on the other line.

I have shared my story with so many, but I would cry and yell "Mommy, I miss you" at the top of my lungs and lay on my bedroom floor until I could barely breathe because my heart hurt so badly. There were many days that I thought I could not go on. Grief often held me hostage for a long time. Even now, it still hurts.

The absence of a loved one is highlighted on days that used to bring joy. Holidays and birthdays are often big reminders that the person that usually sits beside you won't be there. You won't hear their laugh or be able to see them smile. It is these moments that exacerbates your feelings of loss. My first Christmas without my mother, I just gave up and went back to bed. I kept looking for her to come down the stairs and to sit on the sofa for us to watch my son open his gifts and see what Santa Claus brought him. When she never came down, it reminded me that she would never come down those stairs ever again. Things like award ceremonies, baptism, family gatherings, and accomplishments sometimes mean a little less because you wanted your loved one to be present for some of the biggest days of your life. Even weddings, although joyful when two souls are joined together, can be overwhelming because that framed picture or lit memorial candle doesn't take the place of the person that was supposed to be there.

The premise behind this chapter is to encourage you. Even though I shed tears writing this and remembering these difficult moments, my desire is to let you know that grieving is, individual and specific. Please don't let anyone tell 1) You shouldn't grieve. 2) How you should grieve. 3) How long you should grieve. 4) Speaking to a counselor for grief is not acceptable.

It is important for you meet grief where it's at. Essentially, allowing your emotions to come forth, show up in your life, take time when you need it, and acknowledge the space you are in, are ways to cope with grief. Slowly returning back to life as you were is not possible, but creating a new normal is with understanding, time, and patience. I don't have time in this anthology to discuss grief etiquette, but there are certain things that should not be said to a grieving person. Don't say you will offer to help if you really don't plan to. During this difficult time, the bereaved need dedicated and patient people around them. This road is rough and bumpy. A consistent, caring connection can make all the difference. Although you mean well, please don't tell the grief stricken their loved one is in a better place, or they wouldn't come back here if they could. These phrases often heighten the grief because their mind is focused on the absence and the pain. A safe phrase is to say I am sorry for your loss, and I am praying for you, or I am offering my condolences. Grief is met with consistent care, concern, compassion, and understanding. During the grief process, every day can be difficult Take your time and heal the right way. I would like to leave you with this. Emotions matter, feelings matter, the absence does matter, and most importantly **Grief Matters**.

References

Bursack, Carol. "There's a Name for That Wave of Grief That Hits Long after a Loss: STUG." *NewsMd*, 22 Feb. 2022.

Kübler-Ross E. (1969). On Death and Dying. Routledge. ISBN 0-415-04015-9.

New King James Version Bible, 1982), NKJV online. https://biblehub.com/john/11-17-22.htm

New King James Version Bible, 1982), NKJV online. https://biblehub.com/john/11:25,40.htm

New King James Version Bible, 1982), NKJV online. https://biblehub.com/romans/10 Romans 10:9.htm

New King James Version Bible, 1982), NKJV online. https://biblehub.com/romans/10-9.htm Romans 10:13

The Last Mile of the Way. (2016, October 28). Wordwise Hymns. https://wordwisehymns.com/2016/10/28/the-last-mile-of-the-way/

The Lord Will Make a Way Somehow. (n.d.). Hymnary.org. Retrieved September 16, 2022, from https://hymnary.org/text/like_a_ship_thats_tossed_and_driven

Types of Grief: Grief Reactions, Grief Symptoms, and FAQs for Your Own Grief Experience

|Eterneva. (n.d.). www.eterneva.com. https://www.eterneva.com/resources/types-of-grief

Walter, C. A., & McCoyd, J. L. M. (2015). Grief and Loss Across the Lifespan, Second Edition: A Biopsychosocial Perspective. Springer Publishing Company.

About the Authors

Esaunta S. Buncomb

Esaunta S. Buncomb, author and mother of four, is a native of Charleston, South Carolina. Esaunta received her Bachelor of Science in Early Childhood Education from Claflin University in Orangeburg, South Carolina. Her passion for education led her to strive for more and she earned her Master's in Literacy Education with a certification as a reading coach from The Citadel while teaching full-time. Her career spans from working with children in a behavioral health setting to teaching in a classroom which she has done for over 11 years. Just as we all know, life happens when we least expect it or aren't prepared for it! Because of deviations, Esaunta was propelled into writing, becoming an author of two books thus far. The first book, "Far More Precious Than Jewels," addresses the feelings felt through the five stages of grief using the approach of funny short stories and poems. The second book, "For the Love of Daddy," is a children's book that discusses the effects of a child who is experiencing a loss when his parents' divorce and includes activities to help parents/children who are experiencing the same thing. Esaunta now enjoys being an entrepreneur and using her businesses to help promote self-care and addressing the need to grieve after a loss. One component of her brand, Majanel Jewels LLC, is the Grief to Gratitude gift bags that help those who have lost a loved one and/or can be given as a gift to someone who is grieving. Selfish! promotes an essential goal journal and kits for anyone who struggles with self-care. In Esaunta's spare time, and because of her love for children, she offers literacy coaching as she desires to help in the success of those she encounters.

Deidra Shaquana Addison

Deidra Shaquana Addison is the founder of "Everything Deidra" and the non-profit GOALS (Getting Out And Learn Something). She was born January 20, 1980 in Harleyville, SC and raised in St George, South Carolina. She has been serving in the United States Air Force at Joint Base Charleston, as a reservist, since 2014. Deidra is currently employed at Providence/Aston Carter as an Associate Regulatory Assurance Analyst. Deidra also works for SCYAP part-time as a CBS Advocate, in addition to respite for Charles Lea Center twice a week.

She is a graduate of American Military University with a Bachelors and Masters in Psychology. She has also been a Registered Medical Assistant since 2010.Deidra has been a CPR instructor for the American Red Cross since 2014. Deidra has also been a Guardian Ad Litem since 2017. Because of her love for beauty she went to beauty school at Charleston Cosmetology

Institute to become an esthetician. She recently became certified as a Master Life Coach through Transformation Academy. She is a member of the National Notary Association.

She published her first memoir, *"The Bounceback,"* in 2019. She is currently finishing her second memoir, *"Even After The Fact,* in addition to her six book series *"Casey."* Despite her rigorous schedule, Deidra takes full advantage of her free time; she prefers making her own stories-completed with mysterious endings. Deidra also enjoys bartending and cooking. She is happiest with her three children Rasheed, Dejour, and Toure, in addition to her pets Krisette and Cash.

About the Authors

Vera Brown, LPC, CGC

Vera Brown a native of Charleston, SC is a Licensed Professional Counselor, Certified Grief Counselor, Retired Teacher, and Retired School Counselor. She is known for successfully working with children and youth to resolve issues. However, Vera also has a finesse for working with adolescents and adults dealing with grief and loss, ADHD, anxiety, depression, self-esteem issues, stress management and adjustment disorders.

In building relationships with students and their families, she recognized the need for mental health counseling in many of the youth. This was the catalyst that convinced Vera to pursue an additional Master's Degree, in Mental Health Counseling, in addition to her Master's Degree in Education. She's a firm believer in meeting people in whatever state they are in spiritually, emotionally, academically and every other area of their being... because broken crayons can actually color quite beautifully. Vera is also a Co-Author of Amazon's Bestseller anthology entitled "We Are More Than Conquerors." This anthology is a group of women's testimonies written to encourage and inspire others.

Ms. Brown may be reached at via phone at *The Counseling Corner* at 843-270-9929 or via email at ladyvlb@vbcounselingcorner.com or to schedule an appointment.

Dr. Laganna Lawrence

Innovative thought leaders facilitate a unique analeptic to some of society's most detrimental circumstances. Trailblazing a path with that exact intent is the perspicacious professional, Dr. Laganna Lawrence.

Dr. Laganna Lawrence is a native of Anderson, South Carolina. She holds a Doctor of Philosophy in Human Services with a concentration in Social and Community Services from Capella University; a Masters in both Rehabilitation and School Counseling from South Carolina State University; Dual Master of Arts in Human Resource Development & Management from Webster University and a Bachelor of Arts in Sociology from Claflin University. Dr. Lawrence is currently a Professional School Counselor and has over 20 years of experience working in the Human Services arena.

A combination of a successful career with a sincere regard for higher learning and communal involvement is what Dr. Laganna Lawrence embodies. She is an author, co- author, scholar, adroit preceptress, and CEO and Founder of Academic Essentials, LLC; a multi-faceted pedagogy consulting program, providing expert mentorship, advocacy, and facilitation to those looking to advance their lives, through the power of education. Her notable Dissertation Title: Online First-Generation College Students Experiences with Educational Support Services discovered ways to enhance educational support services for online learners transitioning to higher education for the very first time. Dr. Laganna Lawrence also co-authored "Success Chronicles; You Define Your Own Success" Volume 1. This collaboration was ranked as a #1 Amazon International Best Seller and was comprised of 12 Audaciously bold, courageous women who have shattered glass ceilings and crushed every stereotype that says they cannot, should not, and would not succeed. Though an incontestable achiever, Dr. Lawrence's meritorious flex is not found solely in her accomplishments, but rather her legitimacy. Her goal is to live the message she speaks.

Everyone is unique in relation to how they react and process grief, loss, and trauma. Dr. Lawrence specializes in supporting others during times of transition, grief, stress and other critical situations. She understands the physical and mental toll grief can take on a person and has experienced firsthand. Her experiences with witnessing many people on the edge of life and death has taught her how to prioritize living a fulfilled life, even after loss. When Dr. Lawrence is not out changing her world for the better, she is an asset to her local and surrounding communities, a wife and mother to two busy athlete-scholars. She is intentional about making positive memories that will last a lifetime.

If you would like to connect with Dr. Lawrence, she can be emailed at aessentialconsult@gmail.com. Her website is easylearningpro.com.

Dr. Laganna Lawrence. Leader. Educator. Counselor. Philanthropist.

Dr. Shanelle Fields, LPC

Dr. Shanelle Fields is a native of Florence, South Carolina. Her education includes a BA in English Education from College of Charleston, a Masters in School Counseling from the Citadel Military College, and a PhD in Human Services and Counseling from Capella University. From 2002- 2020, she was a middle and high school English teacher and a Professional school counselor.

In November 2018, she completed her supervision to become an LPC and has opened a private practice in Summerville. Dr. Shanelle works to help others who are struggling with issues of self-esteem, grief, anxiety, and depression. Due to her love of education and counseling, she has given many presentations, speeches, and motivational messages to encourage others. Her proudest accomplishment is raising her son as a single parent, working full-time and completing her doctorate. Dr. Fields knows what it is to be in a "stuck place."

In July 2021, Dr. Fields wrote a #1 Amazon Bestselling Book entitled "I Am Enough." This book is a self- reflection and motivation for women and young ladies who are feeling undervalued and passed over. In November 2021, she became an International Bestseller for being a co-author of the book entitled "Women Motivated by Purpose." This anthology seeks to motivate others to live life with purpose. Dr. Fields is also an adjunct professor for Liberty University in their Community Counseling and School Counseling departments. She hones aspiring counselors' skills through her love of God and experience. Additionally, Dr. Fields founded The Healing Group, which is a directory of African American mental health professionals in the state of SC. For further inquiry, the website is www.thehealinggrp.com

Her mottos are "Every day you have the chance to change two people's lives, yours and someone else's and to always remember You Are Enough! If you would like to connect with Dr. Shanelle, she can be emailed at takingthe1ststep31@gmail.com. Her practice website is www.takingthefirststep.net

Author Business

Grief Resources

The Healing Group
www.thehealinggrp.com

Psychology Today
https://www.psychologytoday.com/us

SAMHSA- Substance Abuse and Mental Health Services
Administration
https://www.samhsa.gov/find-help/national-helpline

MUSC Resources
https://muschealth.org/patients-visitors/visitor- information/
pastoral-care/bereavement

American Counseling Association
https://www.counseling.org/knowledge-center/mental-health-
resources/grief-and-loss-resources

Grief Matters with the Authors

www.ingramcontent.com/pod-product-compliance
Lightning Source LLC
Chambersburg PA
CBHW051555120626
46551CB00013B/1523